Wildlife Designs

Wildlife Designs

by Sue Walters

© S.A.WALTERS

Fox
Chapel Publishing

1970 Broad Street • East Petersburg, PA 17520
www.FoxChapelPublishing.com

ISBN 978–1–56523–295–2

Publisher's Cataloging-in-Publication Data

Walters, Sue.

Wildlife designs / by Sue Walters. -- East Petersburg, PA : Fox
Chapel Publishing, c2006.

p. ; cm.
ISBN 978-1-56523-295-2

1. Wildlife art. 2. Wildlife art--Patterns. 3. Animals in art. I. Title.

N7660 .W35 2006
700/.462--dc22   0604

Alan Giagnocavo
Publisher

Peg Couch
Acquisition Editor

Gretchen Bacon
Editor

Troy Thorne
Design and Layout

To learn more about the other great books from
Fox Chapel Publishing, or to find a retailer near you,
call toll-free 1-800-457-9112 or visit us at *www.FoxChapelPublishing.com*.

Note to Authors: We are always looking for talented
authors to write new books in our area of woodworking, design,
and related crafts. Please send a brief letter describing your idea to
Peg Couch, Acquisition Editor, 1970 Broad Street, East Petersburg, PA 17520.

Printed in China
10 9 8 7 6 5 4 3 2

Dedication

To the boys, who continue to look out for me.

To Alison, my Mum, with all my love.

Acknowledgements

To the people who helped with this book:

Barb Kaminski, the calmest person I know. This book would not be the same without you. Thank you for your project contributions; for your writing contribution, photographs, research, and time; for your amazing ideas; and for all of the marathon bull sessions. Lastly, thank you for your undying friendship and encouragement.

Gayle Martin, the most patient person I know. Thank you for your project contribution, your editing, your research, and all of your endless support and help that allow me the freedom to do what I do.

I love you both.

To Dianne Linforth, thank you for doing the quilt project.

To the mob at Fox Chapel Publishing for their guidance, patience, and support.

About The Author

Sue Walters is a self-taught, internationally renowned, and award-winning pyrographic artist. She has won numerous international pyrographic art awards including the 2004 Melbourne Show, 2002 and 2003 Australian Society of Miniature Art International Competition, 2003 Melbourne Working with Wood Woodworking Competition, 2002 Australian National Woodcarving Competition, 2002 Canadian Woodcarving Championships, 2001 Ontario Woodcarvers Association Championships, 2001 Ottawa Woodcarving Championships, and 2001 Hawkwind Wood Carvers Competition. Her first book on pyrography, entitled *Pyrography Workbook*, was published by Fox Chapel Publishing in 2005. Sue also owns a website and online business, *www.suewalters.com*, which offers pyrographic supplies, helpful tips and techniques, and original artwork. Her love of animals, nature, and wildlife has helped to broaden her artistic horizons to include pencil, painting, scratchboard, carving, scrimshaw, engraving, and miniature work. Sue's passion for pyrography and wildlife art continues to this day and is something she hopes to pursue always. A fifth-generation Aussie, Sue was born in 1962 and still calls Australia home.

Contents

Introduction

The appeal of wildlife and nature pictures is universal. Whether it is the intensity of a raptor, the majesty of a buck, the cheekiness of a raccoon, or the peaceful appeal of a loon, pictures of wildlife subjects evoke emotions and pleasure in people that few other images do.

It's natural, then, that crafters and artists would want to translate these images into their own mediums. Unfortunately, they are often deterred because portraying wildlife can prove a daunting proposition to many people.

Wildlife is non-static; it is alive and breathing. Difficulties in portraying wildlife can lie in several areas, including selecting a suitable subject, establishing the essential components of the animal, making a working line pattern, placing the subject in a natural and attractive setting, and adding tone to make the scene come alive.

This book provides you with 30 large North American wildlife designs and 10 border designs. Each design is dynamic and useful to a whole range of crafts and arts, including—but not limited to—pyrography, etching, relief carving, and quilting.

I have included a line and a tonal pattern for each of the 30 large designs in this book. The line patterns show the key elements that make up the design and are intended for ease of transfer, for guidance when applying tone, or for use as a stand-alone pattern. The tonal patterns are designed as a guide to "filling in" the picture so that you can create, if you choose, an ultra-realistic, lifelike image. All tone has been added directly on top of the original line pattern so that the original lines can still be seen, giving you a clear indication of where to place the "darks and lights" of each design.

In addition, this book will show you how to adapt the designs to suit crafts with special pattern needs and how to segment and manipulate the designs to create countless patterns on your own. Transfer advice is also given, along with a chapter dedicated to making the most of the patterns.

It is my hope that you gain inspiration from this book and that you have many enjoyable hours applying these patterns to your particular medium.

—Sue Walters

Using Line Patterns

© S.A.WALTERS

Some of the easiest and most common patterns to use are line patterns. I'm sure you know the type of pattern I'm referring to: bold, black lines on a stark, white background. They are used by all types of crafters, from woodworkers to quilters to painters.

Line patterns show the edges of the objects, the outline of the main groups, and the basic features of a design. They can also be used to indicate important information about a picture, such as the direction of fur or hair (see **Figure 1.1**).

A line pattern can serve two purposes. It can be used to easily transfer the main components of a design to a project before a tonal pattern is used to "fill in" (see Chapter Two, "Using Tonal Patterns," page 5), or it can be used as a stand-alone pattern for a more simplistic, linear result. Following are three ways in which line patterns can be used as stand-alone patterns.

Line patterns for outlines

Some crafts, such as lino printing (a type of printing that uses a scored linoleum block to create an image), dictate that a line pattern is more suitable to use than a tonal pattern. In these types of crafts, only the main features of the pattern should appear in the artwork. Line designs are less complex than tonal patterns and may be preferable for the novice craftsperson to use, no matter what the application (see **Figures 1.2** and **1.3**).

Pen and ink, printmaking, engraving, etching, embroidery, gourd crafting, stamping, woodcarving, pyrography, cross-stitch, and inlay are some examples of where line designs are effective.

Figure 1.1. This line pattern, *Lakeside View*, shows the main components of the picture as well as features such as white cheek pouches and feather groups.

Figure 1.2. The line pattern of the two geese was transferred to a lino block, and carving tools were then used to carve along the lines, recessing them deeper than the surrounding surface.

Figure 1.3. The block is inked and the image is transferred to paper, forming a negative image. The original line pattern creates a simple, yet very effective printed image.

Wildlife Designs

Line patterns for depth perception

Line patterns are also used to transfer designs for relief carving. In relief carving, different areas of the pattern are raised or lowered slightly depending on their proximity to the viewer. This technique creates a dimensional surface and gives the perception of depth to the subject. The same technique, although to a much smaller degree and using a different medium, is used to mint coins. Relief carvers use duplicates of the line pattern to chart the various depth levels needed in the carving (see **Figures 1.4** and **1.5**).

Figure 1.4. Two copies of the line pattern were made for the relief carving of *Lakeside View*. One copy (shown here) was filled in with colored pencil as a reference for the various depths. Each color represents a different depth, with brown being the shallowest and coral being the deepest.

When To Use a Line or a Tonal Pattern

In many arts and crafts, both line and tonal patterns can be used, depending on the desired effect and skill of the artist. How will you know which to choose? Here are some hints.

Use a line pattern if:
- The medium can produce a line (etching, pen and ink).
- You are a novice crafter or artist.

Use a tonal pattern if:
- The medium can produce shades (watercolors, pencil).
- You want to create a more lifelike picture.
- You have experience in your craft.

Figure 1.5. Here, the second copy of the line pattern was transferred to basswood with graphite paper. The lines were initially used as a guide to roughing out the design and were later used as a guide to establish feather groups and other details. The colored pattern was used to gauge depth.

Copyright Sue Walters.

Using Line Patterns

Line patterns for silhouettes

Line patterns can also be used to create silhouettes. A light box or other light source is helpful in this process (see Chapter 5, "Transferring Patterns," page 23). The line pattern is used as a guide to create an outline of the design. The outline is then fully filled in with ink or another pigment to complete the silhouette (see **Figures 1.6** and **1.7**). These silhouette patterns are ideal for crafts such as scroll sawing and paper cutting where the different areas of the image must be separated by connected "rivers" of white space.

Figure 1.6. The original line pattern is used as a basis for making the silhouette. It was placed on a light box with a clean sheet of paper on top of it. The outline of the design was drawn with pen and filled in to create the silhouette.

Figure 1.7. The resulting image is an outline of the objects, as if cast by a shadow. I left little, untouched bridges of white space between the rocks to help distinguish one individual rock from the next.

Using Tonal Patterns

Think of tonal patterns as a guide to "filling in" the picture. Tone refers to the intensity of the colors that make up a picture. Tones in a work of art could be anything from shades of black, as in a pencil sketch, to a variety of shaded colors, as in an oil painting—as long as those shades combine to flesh out the finished piece.

By using the line pattern to transfer the main elements of the design and then using the tonal pattern as a guide to filling it in, you can produce a realistic and lifelike image (see **Figure 2.1**). All of the tonal patterns in this book have been overlaid directly on top of the original line pattern. I have not lightened the lines in any way so that you can clearly see where the tone has been placed. To prevent the pattern marks from showing through the tonal coverage, you may want to lighten the main lines after transfer. I suggest making them light enough to be easily covered by mediums such as woodburning or paint but still dark enough to act as a clear guide. Lightening can be done with an eraser, a tissue, or sandpaper depending on your medium.

Some of the art forms that use tonal patterns are pencil drawing, charcoal drawing, pen and ink, gourd crafting, pyrography, carving, scratchboard, engraving, scrimshaw, etching, cross-stitch, and embroidery.

Figure 2.1. The line pattern is laid down first; then, the tonal pattern is overlaid on the line pattern. Tonal patterns "fill in" the picture to provide a more realistic, lifelike image.

Monochromatic mediums

Tonal patterns can be particularly effective in art forms that use monochromatic (one color) pigments, such as pen and ink, charcoal drawing, and woodburning. Because the tonal pattern shows all of the fur, feather, and other similar detail and because monochromatic mediums use only one color, there's no need for additional reference material (see **Figure 2.2**).

Tonal wildlife patterns are also effective for a craft such as engraving. Transfer is easy if the medium is transparent, such as glass, and there is no need to do an initial line pattern transfer. It's simply a matter of sizing the tonal pattern to fit the project and then taping it to the underside of the glass. The image can then be engraved by following the tonal pattern as seen through the glass (see **Figure 2.3**).

Even though line patterns are often used to transfer a design for use in relief carving, the tonal pattern can also be used as reference to help establish contour, shape, and color. These touches help to add realism to the project (see **Figure 2.4**).

Figure 2.3. The tonal image has been reduced and taped, face up, to the inside of a vase. A rotary tool with a diamond burr attachment is used to engrave the image on the glass.

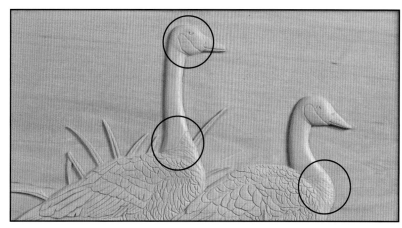

Figure 2.4. Color changes can't be seen in a natural woodcarving, but they can still be depicted. A tonal pattern helps to establish distinctive color areas that would benefit the carving. Here, we see how a gouge has lightly defined the black neck, chest striation, and white cheek pouches.

Figure 2.2. Because pyrography is monochromatic (made of a single color), tonal patterns translate beautifully into this medium. The pattern was transferred using the line pattern and then filled in using the tonal pattern as a guide.

S.A. WALTERS

Using Tonal Patterns

Multichromatic mediums

Tonal patterns can also be used with colored mediums, such as paints, pastels, and folk art/tole art (see **Figure 2.5**). When using a tonal pattern with colored mediums, be sure to gather some additional reference material, such as photographs, to establish the colors you'll need to complete the piece.

Converting Line to Tone

To convert a line pattern to a tonal pattern, use a photograph or a grayscale image from your computer to help you. Start with the dominant features of the pattern's subject. For example, if you are working on a pattern of an eagle, trace the outlines of the face, the beak, the large feather groups, and the feet with a pencil. Then, fill in the smaller details, starting with dark and going to light.

Wildlife Designs

Copyright Barb Kaminski.

Figure 2.5. Mixed mediums can be used to portray a tonal pattern. In this case ink and pastel were combined to create a beautiful, color-filled scene.

Adapting Patterns for Various Arts and Crafts

Pre-designed line or tonal patterns, such as those you find in kits and books, offer an easy way for crafters to make finished works in a variety of mediums. While most patterns can be used quickly "as is" for beautiful results, there are some crafts that require specific pattern modifications before those patterns can be used. Some examples include scroll sawing, stenciling, chip carving, intarsia, quilting, and stained glass/lead lighting.

You may also want to modify a pattern to fit your own creative vision. How you decide to use a pre-designed pattern is restricted only by your imagination. Many craftspeople utilize isolated or combined elements of already-designed patterns as a starting point for portraying their own ideas.

In this chapter, Canadian crafter Barb Kaminski describes how she modified the original *Lakeside View* line pattern (page 38) to produce two distinct segmented pattern styles: freestyle planes (large, open areas) and geometric planes (smaller, more distinguished groupings). These modified designs can be used for a variety of specialized crafts, which require a pattern that is suited to the medium. They can also be used in non-specialized crafts (where a pattern modified to suit the medium is not required) to attain a specific look or style. The novice craftsperson may also find these simplified patterns useful when he or she is learning more about his or her medium.

First, we'll define freestyle and geometric plane patterns in more detail; then, we'll consider what pattern elements to alter. Finally, we'll discuss tracing.

Understanding freestyle or geometric planes

To transform a line or tonal pattern into a series of planes, or shapes, it is best to think in terms of distinctive masses within the picture. These can come in two forms: 1) distinct independent elements, such as body parts and physical items that make up the background, or 2) sections distinguished by a change of color, fur texture and direction, and feather groupings.

In the case of the *Lakeside View* (see **Figure 3.1**), an example of a distinct independent element would be a single reed or a ripple of water. An example of a change in feather groupings can be found in various locations on the birds' backs where the upper back feathers merge into lower back feathers and continue to step down into the tail feathers.

Color distinctions such as the white facial markings can also be found and segmented off to further define the subject and add to the overall picture design. Once these distinctions are recognized, breaking down a pattern into a basic segmented image is not an overly difficult task.

Freestyle Plane Patterns

Freestyle planes follow or outline distinct divisions and groups in a pattern, like body parts or feather groups or background elements. The shapes of the segments are determined by the shapes you are outlining; therefore, they are random in form and follow no standard geometric shape. **Figure 3.2** shows a segmented freestyle plane pattern.

Geometric Plane Patterns

Geometric plane patterns are designed using standard geometric forms—think of triangles for chip carving—to define body parts, feather groups, and other distinct areas of the pattern. **Figure 3.3** shows a segmented geometric plane pattern.

- **Red circle** – Areas of distinctive color sections, such as the white pouch, should be distinguished.
- **Blue circle** – Areas of distinctive color sections, such as the beginning of the black neck, should be distinguished.
- **Green circle** – Distinctive physical sections, such as overlapping feather groups, wings, and main feathers, should be distinguished.
- **Yellow circle** – The outlines of reeds and other distinctive parts of the original pattern should be distinguished.
- **Purple circle** – The outlines of legs, body, and other physical parts should be distinguished.

Figure 3.1. *Lakeside View*, the line pattern of two Canada geese, is cropped for this demonstration to focus on one goose. The purple and yellow circles show the legs and grass, which are distinct individual elements. The red, blue, and green circles show areas that are marked by changes in color and feather groupings.

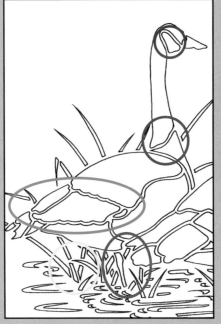

Figure 3.2. The pattern has been altered to a segmented freestyle plane pattern.

Figure 3.3. The pattern has been altered to a segmented geometric plane pattern.

Wildlife Designs

Considerations before starting

The following aspects need to be considered when transforming a line or tonal pattern into a freestyle plane or geometric plane pattern.

1) Which picture elements are best suited for your project?
2) What sizes and shapes should the segmented planes be?
3) How wide should the bridges between segments be?

Which Picture Elements Are Best Suited for Your Project?

The entire original pattern can be used when you are transforming a pattern to freestyle planes or geometric planes, or you may wish to select only part of the design. Prior to beginning the tracing, you should determine which section or sections of the original pattern you would like to use for your project. Many of the patterns provided in this book allow for two or more picture elements to be extracted from the original work and used as stand-alone patterns.

Should you decide to use only a portion of the original pattern, you will need to determine which picture element or elements best suit your project. This is primarily a matter of personal preference, but the size and relative shape of your project may also dictate the most effective area to use. For example, say I want to make an upright (vertical) rubber-stamped card using the *Lakeside View* pattern. In this case, the most appropriate goose to use is the back goose. Its height and stature correspond to the basic shape of the card, and thereby I achieve the best possible balance (see **Figure 3.4**). However, if I were making a horizontal card, the front goose would be best suited to create a sense of proportion and overall balance (see **Figure 3.5**).

Figure 3.4. The taller goose has been selected for this card because of its portrait orientation.

Figure 3.5. The shorter goose has been selected for this card because of its landscape orientation.

Adapting Patterns

Figure 3.6. The small segments that represent the water in this stenciled piece are relatively easy to paint because of the nature of stencil work.

Figure 3.7. Quilting small, curved shapes like the water segments in Figure 3.6 can be difficult. As an option, a patterned fabric was chosen to portray the water in this quilt.

What Sizes and Shapes Should the Segmented Planes Be?

The next important considerations when transforming a pattern are the sizes and shapes of the segmented planes. The decisions made here should be based on what the craft's inherent properties will allow as well as your own personal skill level. For example, with respect to the craft itself, small, finicky segments may be difficult, if not impossible, to work in some projects but may be quite feasible in others. For example, compare the stenciled goose (see **Figure 3.6**) to the quilted geese (see **Figure 3.7**). I can portray the segments of the water ripples quite easily in the stencil, but I would be better off removing them completely from the quilted piece.

Knowing and understanding the limitations of your craft will help you to determine the best elements to alter. But it is also important to understand your own personal skill level. While the more advanced craftsperson may choose to segment a pattern with a number of small planes, for the beginner, it is best to work in simplified, broader planes. By adapting a pattern to best suit your current skill level, you will avoid becoming frustrated by over-complex pattern work, which in turn will lead to a more enjoyable crafting experience and better results.

How Wide Should the Bridges Between the Segments Be?

Even though the segments of a pattern can abut each other, as in quilting, they can also have bridging between the shapes. Bridging is a sort of river of white space that runs between the shapes. Bridging is often added for aesthetic reasons; however, there are certain crafts where bridging is essential, such as scroll sawing and stenciling. Look closely at the stenciled goose in Figure 3.6, and you'll notice bridging between the elements.

The size and width of the bridges should be relative to the size and shape of the actual segments (planes) in your pattern (see **Figure** 3.8). Always keep in mind that the bridges are just as the name reflects: bridgework that holds your segments together. If they become too fine, or narrow, for the material you are using, you run the risk of breaking through the bridge and losing the dividing factor between two planes. In the same respect, if a bridge is too large, the viewer may lose the suggested connection between the planes.

On a project such as the stenciled goose, it is obviously very important that the bridges remain intact and structurally sound in order for the stencil to retain its shape. Conversely, the bridges are of little consequence to the structural integrity of a pattern that's used for quilting and can be eliminated. Bridge width should be dictated by its relative importance to the project at hand. In addition, it should be noted that the overall width of any given bridge within the pattern should be kept as uniform as possible in a freestyle plane pattern to achieve a smooth-looking pattern and create a harmonious flow. In a geometric plane pattern, the bridges may vary in size.

Figure 3.8. The bridges are colored red in this closeup of the segmented plane pattern. Notice how the bridges separate the shapes of the design yet form a completely joined network.

Tracing

Now that you have studied your pattern and you know what shapes you want to turn into planes (either freestyle or geometric), the simplest way to create a new pattern is to trace the original one. Use a transparent tracing paper or, if your paper is heavy, use a light box to project the original pattern through (see **Figure 3.9**). Then, trace only the sections you require for your finished piece based on the earlier discussions.

Note that either a line pattern or a tonal pattern can be used as the original piece from which to work. The line pattern is easier to

see in its simplified form, but the tonal pattern provides extra detail regarding changes in color and fur or feather detail.

As you can see, the combinations and variations for pattern adaptation are without limitations. On the following pages, I have included a couple of projects and their altered patterns for your reference. They certainly do not include all that could be done to make the pattern your own. Play with thoughts and ideas—what may or may not work with your specific craft—and the possibilities become endless. Most importantly, have fun!

Figure 3.9. A light box is ideal for selecting which elements to trace when drawing a segmented pattern.

Examples of freestyle plane patterns

Lakeside View (original pattern on page 38) was adapted into a freestyle plane pattern to be used in crafts requiring larger, independent, segmented planes such as stencil work, stained glass, rubber-stamping, quilting, and enameling. Crafts such as these rely upon the most fundamental shapes in a design to portray a larger picture.

As you look at the finished examples and their patterns in **Figure 3.10** to **Figure 3.12**, note the various planes selected to represent the freestyle planes. You'll see that individual picture elements such as reeds and water ripples have been selected and used to represent individual planes. In addition, the geese themselves have been broken into planes based on both color separation and feather groupings.

Also note the basic uniformity of the bridges between the planes. Can you see how each plane's profile complements its adjacent plane and how the bridge width remains a constant? The individual pieces should look as though they will mate together like the pieces of a jigsaw puzzle. This creates a harmonious flow to the overall pattern.

Figure 3.10. Numerous water ripples appear below the geese in the original pattern. When I altered this pattern for the stained glass project, I used only one goose. I reduced the number of ripples and magnified them to allow for the limitations of the medium.

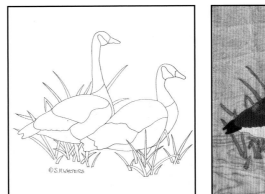

Figure 3.11. This freestyle plane pattern has the same broad shapes as the pattern above, but it's missing the bridges. Because shapes in quilting can abut each other, the original line pattern was modified to remove the bridges.

Figure 3.12. A freestyle plane pattern can simply be colored in with various mediums for great effect.

Figure 3.13. When drawing the goose, the basic outline was traced, breaking the line at various points to allow for smaller, easier-to-carve pieces. (Note the small breaks in the neck and body outline.) The main body of the goose is viewed in feather masses, and back and tail feather groups are stylized into basic triangles and diamonds; chest feathers are portrayed as gentle C shapes. The reeds and water ripples are treated as individual elements. Bridgework in chip carving need only be considered in regards to its aesthetic appearance and its basic strength integrity with respect to adjacent chips to be made.

Figure 3.14. The original pattern was further adapted for scroll saw work. Here, bridgework becomes more important as these joining spaces are once again truly functional bridges that secure planes and keep the finished piece from falling apart. For the scrollwork, a variation on the neck and head of the goose provides for a more dramatic and punchy look. The neck and head section was treated as a freestyle plane and cut out as a large mass, creating a very dramatic look.

Examples of geometric plane patterns

Even though a geometric plane pattern can be used in any craft, **Figures 3.13** and **3.14** feature crafts requiring smaller geometrically shaped planes, such as chip carving, scroll sawing, and stenciling.

The geometric plane pattern is a more stylized version of the original pattern than the freestyle pattern. Some crafts, such as chip carving, require these smaller specific shapes as an inherent part of the craft itself. Other crafts, such as scroll sawing, are merely made more interesting and develop an entirely different aesthetic look through the use of smaller stylized planes.

For these examples, I chose to extract the back goose from *Lakeside View* combined with the foremost group of reeds to create a stylized geometric pattern. By combining two separate picture elements, I was able to maintain the overall balance set forth in the original pattern. (This is another example of taking various elements of a pattern and combining them to form an entirely different design.) The pattern was primarily designed with chip carving in mind, since this craft requires specific shapes such as diamonds and triangles to be effectively carried out.

Modifying Patterns

Without the means to copy, resize, and manipulate the patterns in this book, their use would be restricted to projects that could accommodate the exact size and orientation of the original patterns. Being able to change the patterns' size and orientation makes them suitable to use on a far greater range of projects.

Tools

There are several ways to change the size and orientation of a pattern. Each has its own benefits and detriments, ranging from time and convenience to cost. Choose the method that is right for you.

Photocopy Machine

Copies of the original pattern can be made using a photocopy machine. Depending on the copy machine, the image can be resized, rotated, flipped, and adjusted for contrast and brightness. Printouts are then made for use on your project.

Home Computer

Many people who have a home computer also have a scanner. A scanner simply connects to your computer and makes digital copies of flat objects, such as a sheet of paper. This digital copy is sent to your computer where it can be saved and stored as a digital image. This digital image can then be sent to your printer, which will print as many copies of the image as you like. (**Note:** To print a good-quality copy of a scanned image, it is best to scan at a setting of 200dpi or greater—300dpi being standard.)

The beauty of digital images is that they can be resized and manipulated in various ways by the means of imaging software. Imaging software can be bought, but many computers have basic imaging software installed already. Most scanners, printers, and digital cameras come packaged with some variety of imaging software. (**Note:** Free imaging software can also be found on the Internet.)

Imaging programs can vary in the variety of tools and special effects they have, but even the most basic will allow the resizing, rotating, flipping, selecting, erasing, and cropping of an image. These tools alone will allow the original pattern to be manipulated in ways that will increase its potential use.

Paper and Pencil

As I mentioned in the previous chapter, paper and pencil can be a very efficient way to transform a pattern. This method can also be used to change the size and orientation of an original pattern. While this method is not as common as digital methods today, some artists and crafters find that they enjoy the hands-on aspects of using pencil and paper to change their patterns. Others turn to paper and pencil because they don't know how to use a computer or can't afford one. Whatever your reason, here are some quick tips to using this tried-and-true method.

Tracing of an original pattern can be done by using transparent paper made just for this purpose. If you are using heavier paper, try putting the original on a light table or taping it to a lighted window. Place the heavier paper on top of the original pattern, and the light from the light table or the window should provide enough contrast to allow you to trace the pattern. This method allows you to flip patterns and isolate or combine certain areas.

To enlarge a pattern with paper and pencil, use graph paper and transfer a small portion of the image to a larger block. This method is time consuming, but it allows you to make your own additions, subtractions, or alterations to the pattern as you go. If you have access to an overhead projector or an art projector, you could also enlarge the pattern by projecting the image on a wall or on your medium, adjusting the size of the projection to fit the desired area. Then, simply trace the projected image.

Examples of manipulation

To give you an example of what can be done, I scanned a couple images (see **Figure 4.1** to **Figure 4.6** on this page and the next) into a computer and manipulated the saved images with imaging software. As you can see, one pattern can quickly multiply as you apply various techniques.

Basic ways to manipulate a pattern

Resize	Reduce or enlarge the size of the image.
Flip, or Mirror	Flip an image so that it's a horizontal reflection of its original self.
Rotate	Rotate the image or straighten a crooked image.
Isolate	Select and isolate a part of the image. Parts of patterns can also be isolated to be used in conjunction with other images or can be used alone. For example, the main wildlife subject could be removed so that the supporting scenery is isolated for use with a different animal.
Erase	Erase (rub out) parts of the image.
Crop	Another way of selecting an area of the image.

Figure 4.1. The original scanned image of *Duo*. The two wolves placed side-by-side create a landscape orientation, ideal for wide projects.

Figure 4.2. The original image was cropped to include just the wolf on the right. A digital eraser from the imaging program was used to rub away the extra parts of the rock, leaving the wolf and a portion of the rock isolated as a new design. Isolating one wolf changes the orientation of the pattern to a portrait shape, making it more appropriate for a tall, narrow project.

Figure 4.3. I flipped the drawing in the imaging program to create a mirror image of the wolf on the right. This gives the appearance of a new design because the wolf faces the opposite way. Flipping a design can also help a pattern suit a project better. For example, the wolf can appear either on the left or the right of a clock project. If the resulting illustration is a bit unbalanced, you can straighten it out with the rotating tool.

Figure 4.4. The original design shows a fox in front of a rustic fence. By removing the fox, the fence can be easily used alone or in another design. (The fence could also be removed if you want to use the fox alone.)

Figure 4.5. Here, after scanning the design, I have edited the picture on a computer by using the "erasing" tool of an image software program. I have removed the image of the fox and filled in the lines of the fence post and rail that were originally obscured.

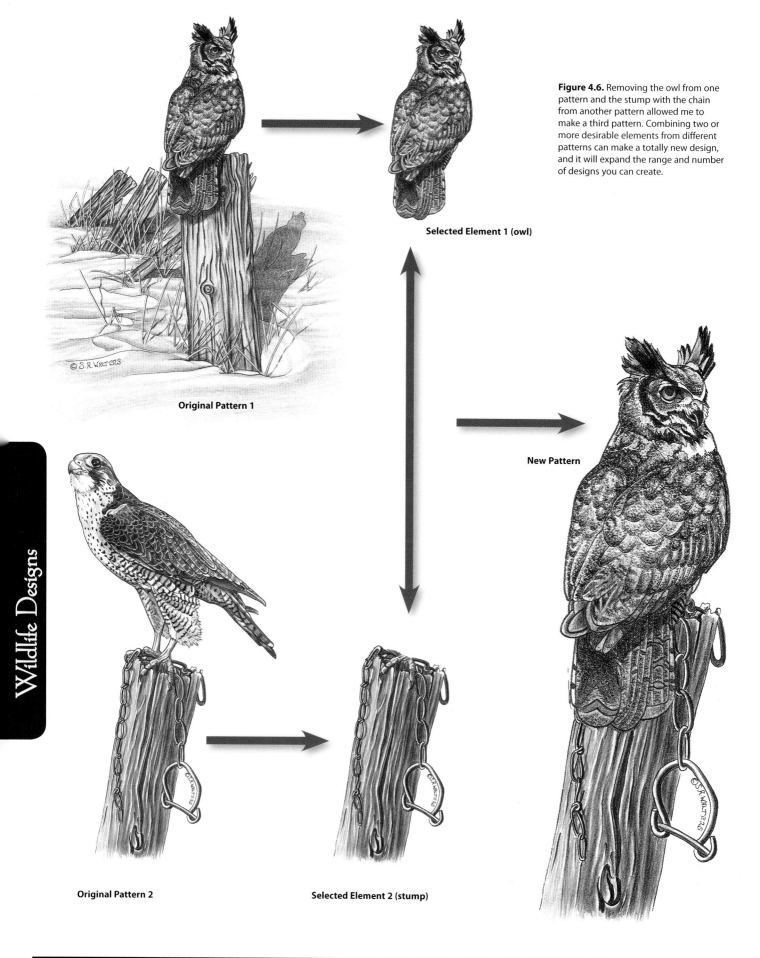

Figure 4.6. Removing the owl from one pattern and the stump with the chain from another pattern allowed me to make a third pattern. Combining two or more desirable elements from different patterns can make a totally new design, and it will expand the range and number of designs you can create.

Selected Element 1 (owl)

Original Pattern 1

New Pattern

Wildlife Designs

Original Pattern 2

Selected Element 2 (stump)

Other image enhancements

Many imaging programs come with tools, called filters, that allow you to alter an image in unusual ways. Depending on your software, these filters can number just a few in basic programs to hundreds in advanced programs.

In **Figures 4.7** to **4.10** on this page and the next are just a few samples of a digitally altered *Lakeside View.* Please note that the names of the filters alter from program to program. Below, I've described the filters using their basic functions.

Figure 4.7. A two-bit filter reduces the complexity of the original tonal range, leaving black and white with no tones in between. This filter could be of benefit to the novice or for certain crafts, such as pen and ink or printmaking.

Figure 4.8. Colorizing will change the original black image to another color. This filter may be especially useful for those working in monochrome (one color).

Figure 4.9. A negative filter is an excellent way to establish what areas need to be removed from linocuts, woodblocks, and rubber stamps.

Figure 4.10. A filter called "hot wax" in my imaging program allows me to see what my image will look like on different colored papers or other surfaces.

Wildlife Designs

Transferring Patterns

N ow that you have a pattern that's been transformed and enlarged or reduced to the correct size, how do you transfer it to your work? Because the line patterns have been produced showing the key elements that make up the design, they are the most suitable patterns to use when transferring the design. The tonal patterns can also be used but are not quite as easy to work with.

There are various methods that can be used to transfer patterns. The method chosen will often depend on the material to which the pattern is being applied. Following are several means of transfer, but this is not an exclusive list. Your own craft may well have a preferred method of transferring patterns, and you could easily follow that established practice when using the designs in this book.

To prevent damaging the original patterns in the book, and for ease of use, a copy should be made to use for the transfer. This could be done by using a photocopy machine, scanning the image into a computer and printing a copy, or manually tracing the design.

Methods of transferring patterns

Graphite paper can be placed under a copy of the pattern and then drawn over, transferring the image to the project below (see **Figure 5.1**). A hard lead pencil can be used, but a red ballpoint pen is recommended so you can tell what lines you've traced. Graphite paper comes in various colors, so it is useful in transferring patterns to dark-colored surfaces. Graphite is ideal for painted projects because it can be erased and has little or no show-through. It also won't bleed on contact with heat, and for this reason, graphite is recommended for pyrographic projects.

Penciling the back of the pattern is another way to use graphite. The original pattern should be photocopied or scanned and printed. The reverse side of the printout is rubbed all over with a soft lead pencil. The rubbed side is placed on the project, and the design is traced with a hard pencil or pen, transferring the design via the rubbing.

Tape tracing paper over the pattern and trace the image with a felt pen. The resulting tracing can have pencil rubbed over the back and can be transferred via the above method. Alternatively, graphite or carbon paper can be used to transfer the traced pattern.

A light box or another light source can be used to illuminate the pattern from below. The design is placed over the light source and a clean sheet of paper or fabric or whatever medium you are using is placed on top. The image is seen through the top sheet and can then be copied. A window can work equally as well.

Carbon paper can be placed under a copy of the pattern and then drawn over, transferring the image to the project below. A hard lead pencil can be used, but a red ballpoint pen is recommended so your lines stand out from the pattern. Carbon comes in either black or blue and can be used for crafts such as relief carving. Because it will bleed on contact with heat, carbon paper is not recommended for pyrographic projects.

Spirit transfer can be used to transfer photocopied or laser printed images. Place the printed copy face down on the project and rub mineral spirits on the back (see **Figure 5.2**). The transferred image is a reverse of the original. This method can be used on crafts such as relief carving, pyrography, and chip carving.

Heat transfer can be used if a pattern is made with a laser printer or a photocopier. Place it face down, and, when heat is applied to the back, a reverse image will be transferred to the surface underneath. A clothes iron, soldering iron, or pyrographic shader can be used to directly apply heat (see **Figure 5.3**). This method of transfer can be used on crafts such as relief carving, pyrography, and chip carving.

Direct copying can be used if the material you are using for a project is transparent (such as glass or Plexiglas). You can tape a copy of the pattern to the opposite side of the desired work area (see Figure 2.3 on page 7).

Pouncing is a method of transfer where holes are closely pricked through lines of the pattern with a pin or pouncing wheel. The perforated design is placed on the project, and then pencil, charcoal, pastel, or other colored dust is pushed through the holes with a brush or cloth.

Glue can hold a pattern to a project. The pattern can be glued directly to the project. This is a useful transfer method for crafts such as scroll sawing and quilting.

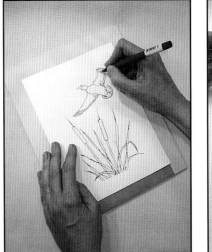

Figure 5.1. Graphite paper can be an easy way to transfer your pattern to your material. Simply place it under a copy of the pattern and then draw over it. A red pen makes it easy to see which lines you've traced.

Figure 5.2. Spirit transfer can be used for photocopied or laser printed images. Simply place the printed copy face down on the surface and rub mineral spirits on the back. The transferred image is a reverse of the original. To get an exact copy of the original, flip the image before transferring.

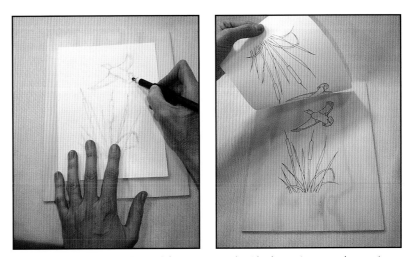

Figure 5.3. Heat transfer can be used if a pattern is made with a laser printer or a photocopier. Place the pattern face down and apply heat to the back. Here, I am using a pyrographic shading nib to heat the back of the pattern.

Project Gallery

In this book, I wanted not only to provide a collection of quality nature patterns, but also to show the reader that any of these designs can be applied to suit their own particular art or craft. With this in mind, I gave the same pattern, *Lakeside View* (found on pages 38 and 39), to a group of people and asked them to apply the pattern to their favorite crafts. The end results showed that either the line or tonal pattern (or both) could be successfully used to create several different craft projects, using a wide range of mediums.

All-around craftsperson Barb Kaminski made stamps from the design and used them to create cards. She also chip carved a plaque (using the carving as the basis for a peg board), drew a picture in pen and ink, and made stencils to decorate a serving tray. Finally, she carved a lino block from the design and used this to print a linocut picture. Scroll saw craftsperson Gayle Martin used the pattern to create a scroll saw silhouette, and Dianne Linforth took the design and applied it to her favorite craft, quilting. Lastly, I applied the design to pyrography, relief carving, glass staining, and tole painting.

Guest Artist Biographies

Dianne Linforth – A ten-year quilting veteran, Dianne lives in Melbourne, Australia, with her husband, John, and three children. After living in the U.S. for 18 months, Dianne's existing interest in quilting ignited, and she has been passionately involved ever since. She is a member of the Essendon Quilters and the Willows Quilting Group, Melton, and is a past member of the Northwestern Suburban Quilting Guild, Chicago. Dianne has exhibited extensively and has been featured in *Australian Patchwork and Quilting* magazine.

Barb Kaminski – Barb was born in 1961 in a small town in Ontario, Canada, and is the youngest of ten siblings. She recently retired from a career in quality control in the field of manufacturing. She enjoys spending time dabbling in pyrography, woodcarving, woodworking—and online chatting with author Sue Walters, her best friend in the "Land Down Under." Barb is currently a member of The Owl's Nest Carving Club. Barb lives with her husband, Frank, and their dog, Cody. She happily remains a small-town girl.

Gayle Martin – Gayle, born in 1961, has had a keen interest in woodworking most of her life. She took up the scroll saw three years ago, and it soon became her favorite hobby. She is a member of the Australian Scroll Saw Network as well as various online scroll saw groups. Gayle lives in Melbourne, Australia.

S.A.WALTERS

Sue Walters

For a more realistic picture, I used the tonal pattern as my guide to woodburning this design. I used the line pattern to transfer the image to the 11" x 7.5" basswood round. (The line pattern is simpler to transfer and shows me all of the necessary elements of the picture.) I did this by resizing a printout of the pattern and using black graphite to transfer. After transfer, I used a skew to burn along all of the lines. I then referred to the tonal pattern to fill in the picture using a shading nib and a writing nib.

Relief Carving

Sue Walters

North American wildlife subjects are a favorite to relief carve. I transferred a line pattern to a piece of 11" x 8.5" basswood using black graphite paper and a red pen. I also used a duplicate line pattern to color a map, indicating the depth I would need to carve each section in relation to each other. After transfer, I used traditional methods and hand tools to relief carve the design. I primarily used the line pattern as a guide to roughing out edging while referring to the tonal pattern to determine contours, shape, and color. For example, the distinctive color of the white cheek pouch, the white lower neck, and the lower neck striations were indicated with carving.

Dianne Linforth

In quilting, shape and material selection are all-important. Quilter Dianne Linforth chose to use the segmented freestyle pattern, which provided the group shapes needed to depict the design in material. The gaps between each segment were deleted so that each shape/piece of material could be sewn flush next to its neighbor. The pattern and color of the fabric were skillfully selected to represent the color and texture of each distinctive segment of the design. This is especially evident in the material representing the backs and the white parts of the geese, as well as the sky and the water. The material backing the piece has a duck pattern on it, in keeping with the water bird theme.

Rubber Stamp

Barb Kaminski

The two rubber stamps were created using two separate parts of the segmented freestyle plane pattern: one tall goose pattern and one shorter goose pattern. The geese patterns were sized on the computer to accommodate a 5" x 7" rubber printmaking block. Although graphite paper could be used to transfer the image to the block, Barb found that the transfer was not very clean. Instead, she found that the best way to create a clear image was to scribble on the back of the sized pattern with a soft 8B pencil, covering the entire surface with a coat of heavy graphite. The pattern was then taped (graphite side down) to the block and traced over in pen, leaving a defined graphite image on the rubber block. The rubber blocks were then cut away with a lino cutter, producing the stamps themselves. To add some flare to the shorter goose stamp, she abstracted the background area of the block to create a mottled look when inked over and stamped onto paper cards. The taller goose was used to print the vertical-style card because its overall height and stature were best suited for this shape. Alternately, the shorter goose was used to stamp the horizontal-style card with the mottled finish creating a fuller image. The cards were further dressed with envelopes, text, and colored paper to complement the stamped images.

Project Gallery

Barb Kaminski

The linocut and print were created from the original line pattern. Since a linocut is just that—a series of cut lines in a linoleum block—there was no need to alter the pattern in any way. The block used was an 8" x 10" linoleum block, so sizing was not an issue either. Barb chose to use the pattern exactly as is, using graphite paper to transfer the picture onto the block. Note that, since she used the image as is for the transfer to the lino block, the print itself is mirrored. If she had wanted the print to be orientated exactly as the pattern is, it would have been necessary to reverse the pattern prior to transferring it to the linoleum block. This method can also apply to woodcuts and other forms of printing.

Scroll Saw

Gayle Martin

Because bridges (uncut pieces of wood) are needed to hold together a scroll saw picture, the geometric plane pattern was the most suitable for this use. Gayle Martin started with a pattern developed for chip carving, but she did alter it slightly so she could cut away the head and neck area, making it black, and leave the cheek pocket uncut, making it white. She also decided to remove the veins from the reeds in the original pattern because they would be very awkward to scroll and likely to break. She then scanned the pattern and used a computer to alter its size to fit the 25 x 20 cm (10" x 8") hoop pine plywood she was using. She transferred the design by printing the pattern and sticking it onto the wood using an adhesive spray. Once the design was cut using a scroll saw, she removed the pattern and sanded. The whole piece was then backed by a black matting to create a black-and-white picture.

Sue Walters

I used the basis of the segmented freestyle plane pattern for this stained glass project. I could have also used the same pattern without bridge gaps, instead using the piping to divide the planes. I soon realized that the shapes were too detailed and close together to be successful, so I modified the pattern to make the shapes larger and more manageable. (This pattern could also be used for other decorative glass projects, such as lead lighting.) Because the glass is transparent, I printed a copy of the adapted pattern and taped it face up on the underside of my project glass. I then used this as a guide to piping the "leadlight" edges. Once the piping had set, I removed the pattern and applied the glass stain.

Chip Carving

Barb Kaminski

The chip carving was created using the segmented geometric plane pattern. Barb sized the pattern on the computer to an approximate 8" x 8" image to accommodate the piece of 8" x 12" basswood used in this pegboard project. The pattern was transferred using graphite paper onto the basswood, placing the image slightly higher than center to allow for the addition of shaker pegs to the plaque. Since this pattern was specifically adapted for chip carving, the actual carving was simply a combination of freeform and chip carving techniques. Upon the completion of the carving, she drilled holes along the bottom profile of the plaque and added three shaker pegs to create a small pegboard. The project was topped with a Varathane matte finish.

Wildlife Designs

Stencils

Barb Kaminski

Barb Kaminski modified the original line pattern to create a new pattern that has segmented planes divided by bridges, ideal for cutting a stencil sheet. She selected the foremost goose for the project. This is a good example of dividing a pattern or selecting an element from a pattern that best suits your project or craft. The stencil was created using the segmented freestyle plane pattern. She reduced the goose pattern size on the computer to accommodate the 6"-square terra cotta tiles. Rather than tracing the image onto the stencil blank (Mylar), the reduced pattern was actually adhered with a low-tack glue directly onto the stencil to be cut. She then cut out the pattern using a fine-tipped X-acto blade. The completed blank was used to stencil the image onto the two tile squares, which were later built into the wooden tray. Since a stencil can be used in either direction, she could stencil two opposing geese, creating an overall balance and symmetry to the tray.

Ink and Pastel

Barb Kaminski

A combination of both line and tonal patterns can be used in conjunction for many arts and crafts. Here, Barb Kaminski used the line pattern to transfer and line the design and the tonal pattern to help fill in the picture. The ink and pastel picture was created using the original line pattern to transfer the pattern to a canvas panel using graphite paper. Permanent ink markers were used to draw over the graphite image. The tonal pattern was then used as a guide to inking in individual feathers and the head/neck area, giving the geese some additional depth. After all of the ink work was complete, the canvas was sprayed with a light matte tole finish to prevent smearing. The basic feather coloring was created using both the tonal pattern and some color photos of Canada geese. The brown and white areas of the feathers were colored in using oil pastel pencils. Barb then colored and blended the reeds, water, and sky area with different colored oil pencils. Finally, the entire picture was once again sprayed over with a tole finish.

Tole Painting/Folk Art

Sue Walters

Tonal patterns can be used for tole painting/folk art. Some additional supporting reference material may be needed to establish the color values of the subject. For this project, I referenced some photos of geese. I used graphite paper to transfer the line pattern to the gourd. I then used a woodburner with a skew nib to outline all of the lines. This gave me distinct, clean, permanent lines, which I could then paint between with acrylic paint. I finished the piece with an acrylic-based spray varnish.

Patterns

In making these patterns, I tried to create designs that not only showed popular North American wildlife, but also placed each subject in a harmonious setting. The tonal pattern has been drawn directly over the line pattern to allow the user to easily see how the "clothes" of tone fit over the "skeleton" of the line pattern.

Lakeside View

Canada Geese

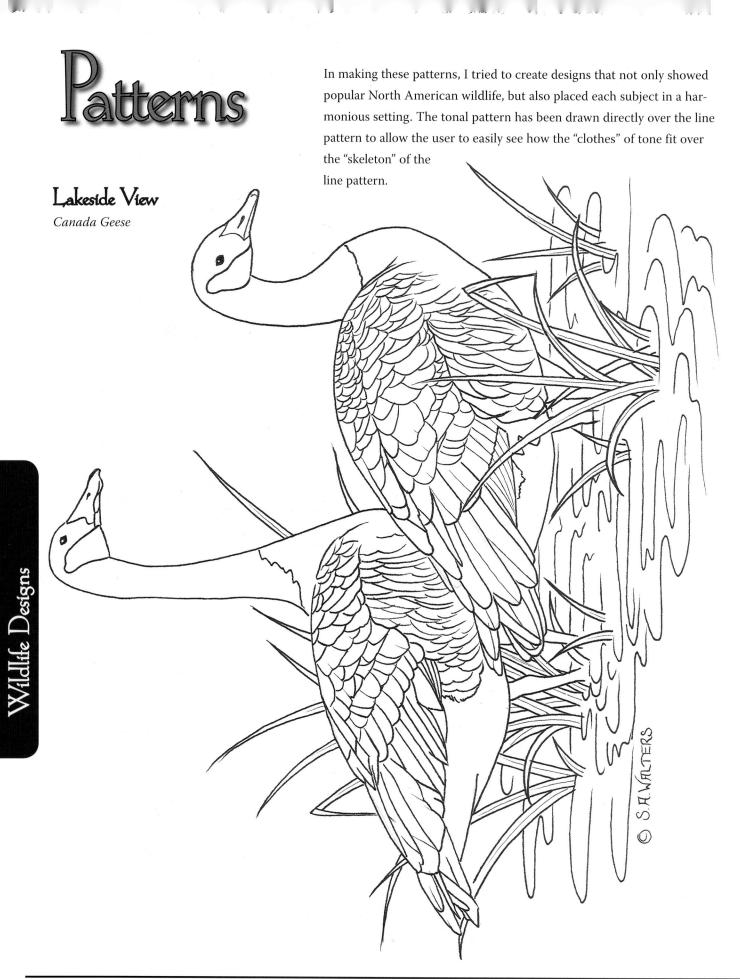

© S.A. WALTERS

© S.A.WALTERS

Call of the Golden Eagle

Golden Eagle

© S.IRVIETERS

Framed

Barn Swallows

© S.R. WALTERS

Home on the Range

Pronghorn Buck

©S.A.WALTERS

©S.A.WALTERS

Under the Wire

Sparrows

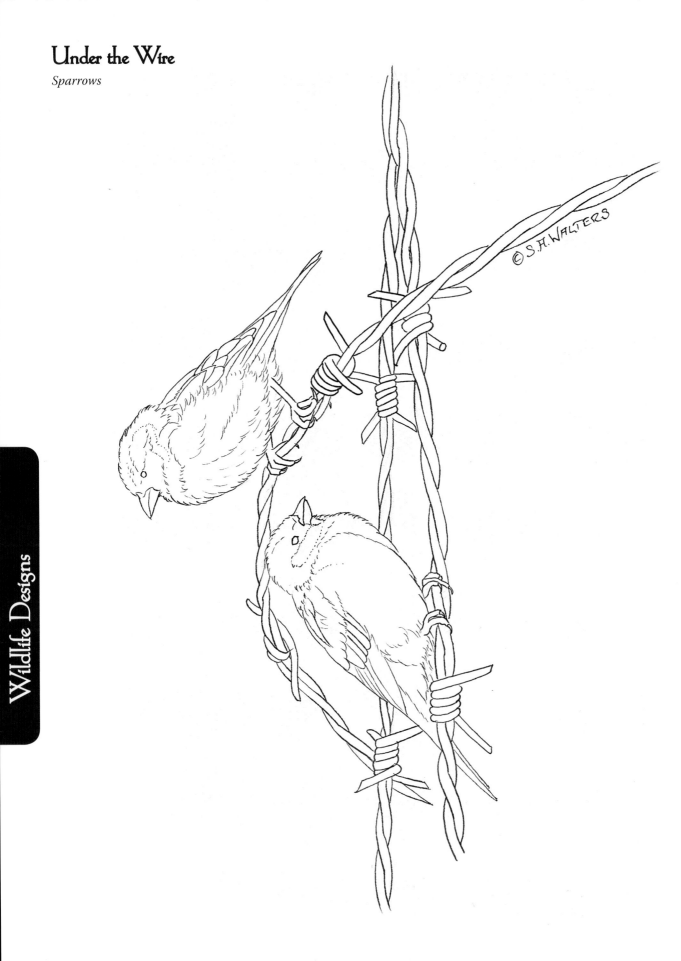

©S.A.WALTERS

Big Red and Mate

Red Squirrels

Wildlife Designs

Jane Doe

Deer

Wildlife Designs

©S.A.WALTERS

©S.A.WALTERS

Lookout Post

Peregrine Falcon

Waterloo County Sentinel

Horned Owl

© S. A. WALTERS

©S.A.WALTERS

John Deer

Mule Deer

© S.A. WALTERS

Duo

Wolves

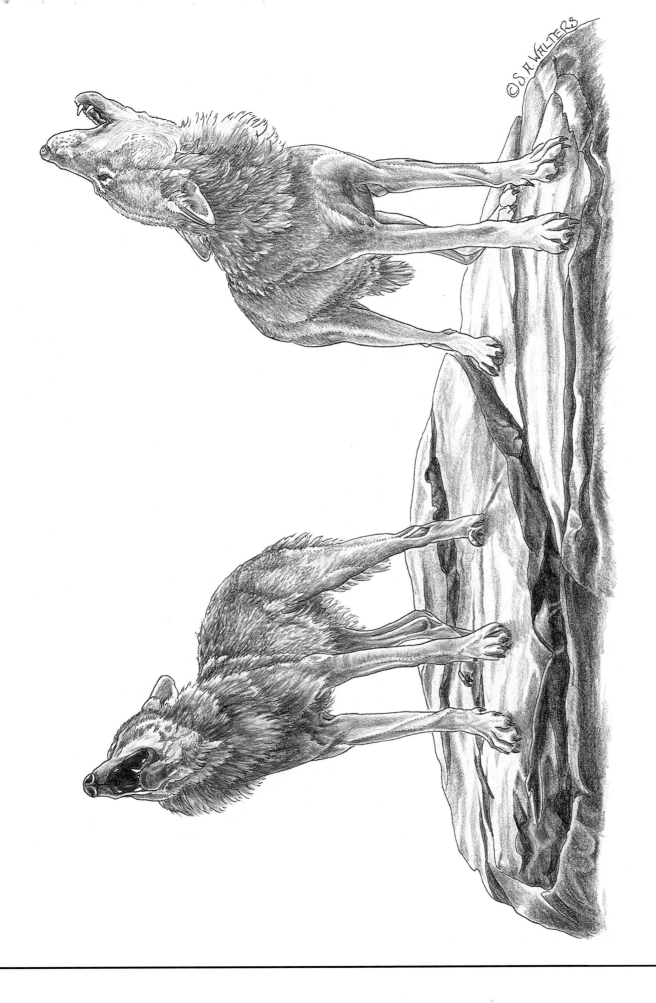

Flutter By

Butterfly

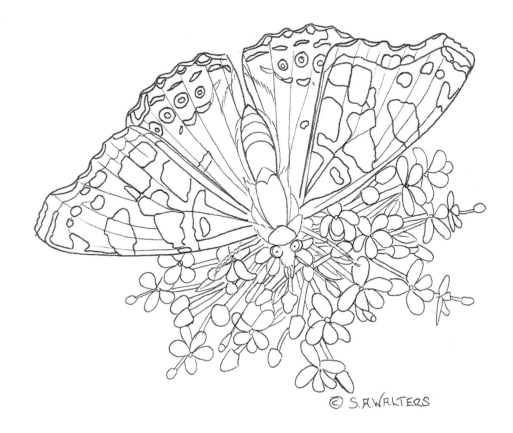

© S.A.WALTERS

© S.A.WALTERS

Happy Wanderer

Wanderer Butterfly

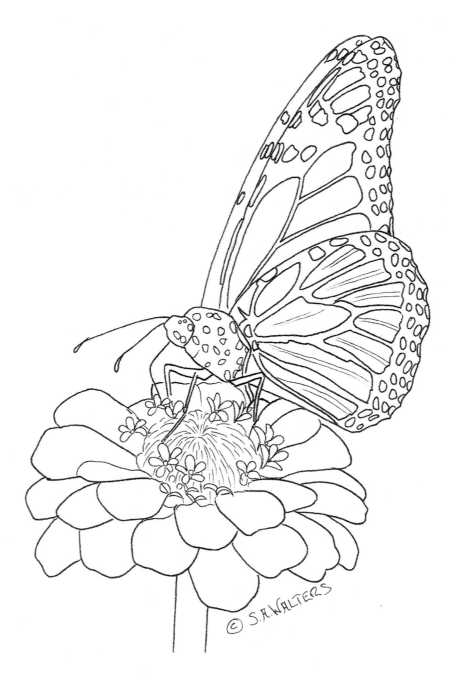

© S.A.WALTERS

© S.A. WALTERS

On the Rocks
Polar Bear

©S.A.WALTERS

©S.A.WALTERS

Majesty
Bald Eagle

Dinner for Two
Chickadees

©S.H.WALTERS

The Long Walk Home

Red Fox

Wildlife Designs

Left Behind

Cougar

Chip and Dale

Chipmunks

Focused

Cooper's Hawk

Double Billing
Ducks

©S.A.WALTERS

Horn of Plenty
Bighorn Sheep

Owl Be Seeing You

Barn Owl

© S.A.WALTERS

Hangover

Raccoon

Shawn Sheep

Dall Sheep

©S.A.WALTERS

©S.A.WALTERS

In the Drink

Moose

Wildlife Designs

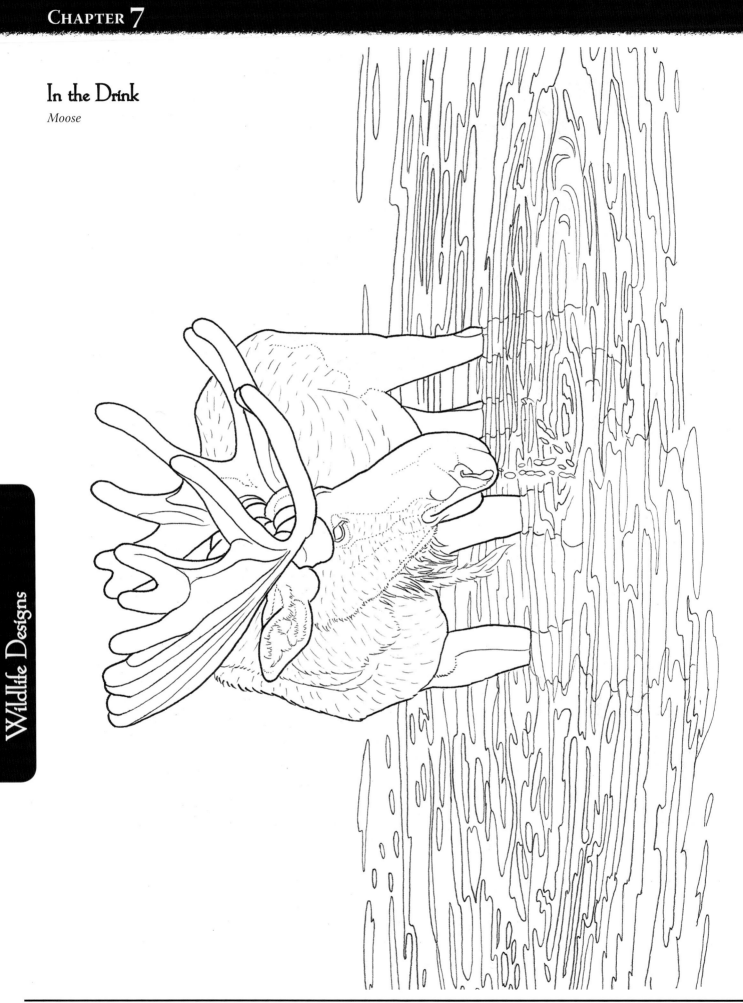

©S.A.WALTERS

Claire the Loon

Common Loon

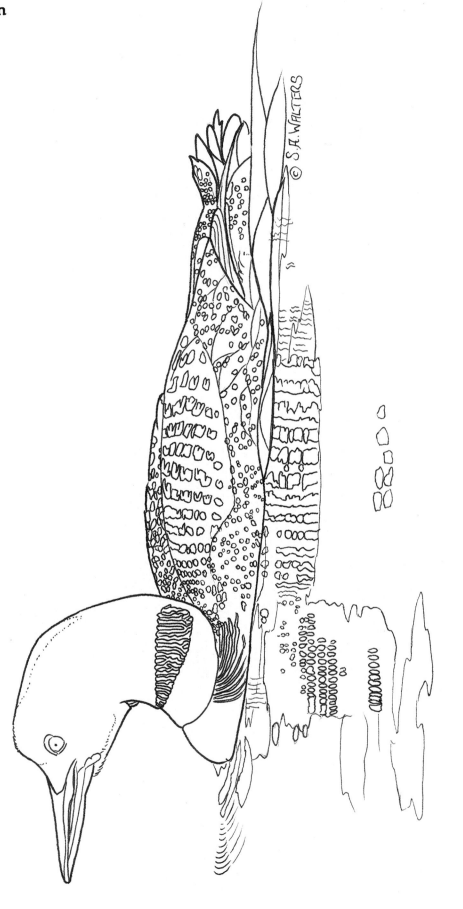

© S.A. WALTERS

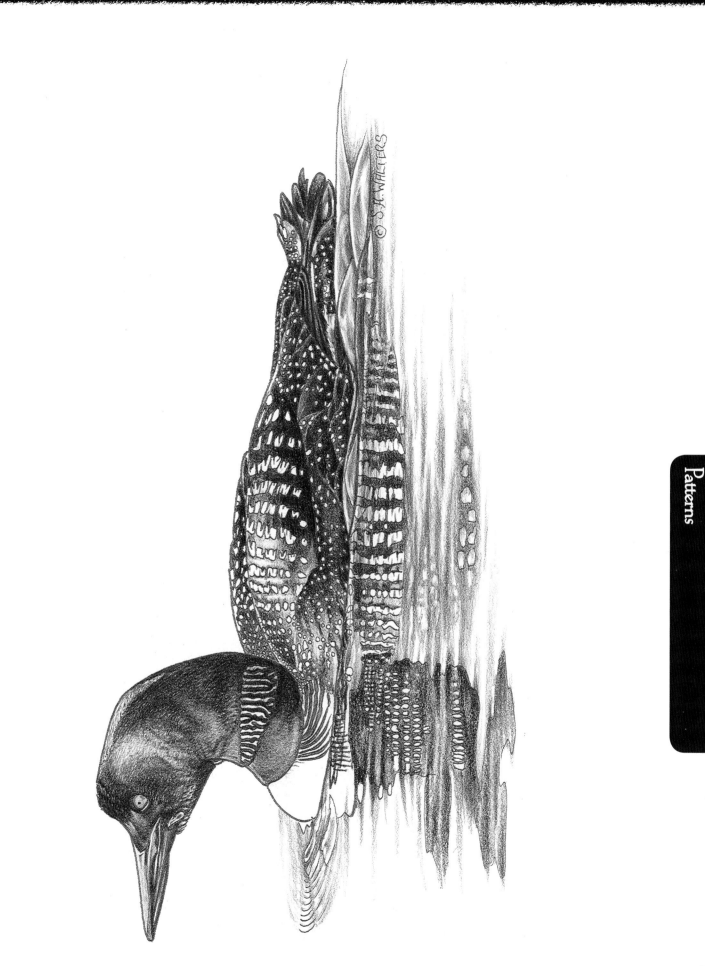

Buffalo Bill

Bison

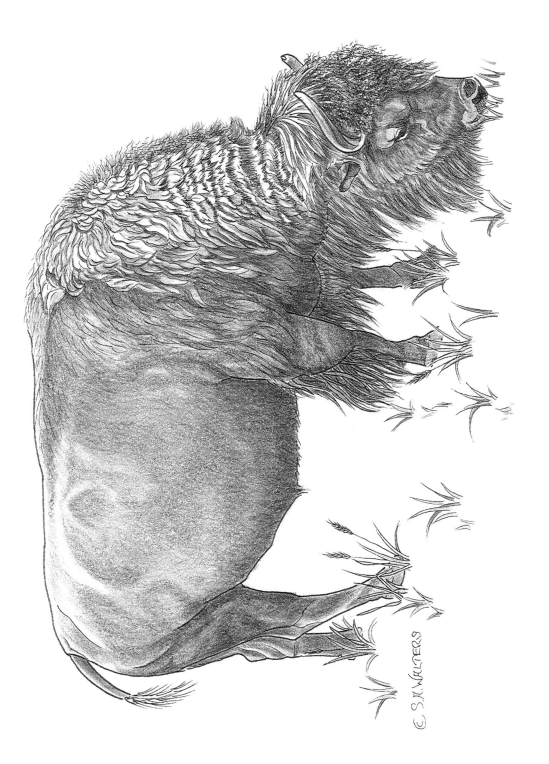

© S.A.WALTERS

Mountaineer

Mountain Goat

©S.A.WALTERS

© S.A.WALTERS

Bugle Boy

Elk

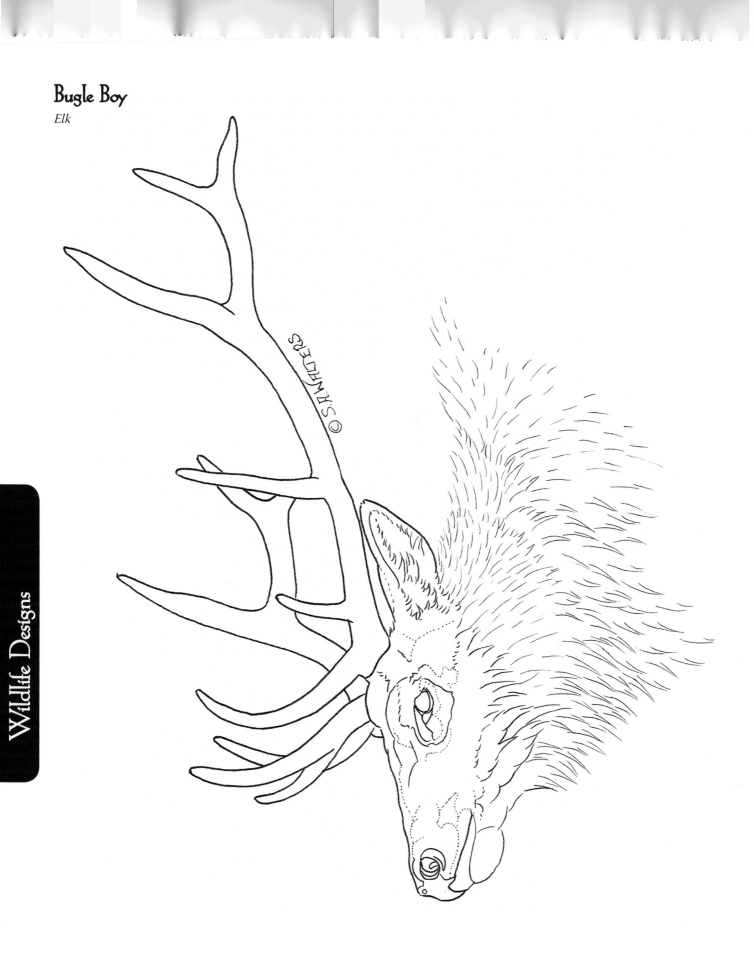

Wildlife Designs

Corners and Borders

The following border designs can be used for adding simple, yet effective, decoration on the corners and edges of objects. They are ideal for decorating a myriad of projects, such as frames, peg boards, signs, mantels, and furniture, and can be used in a wide range of crafts.

Two border designs have been burnt onto this picture frame to add a decorative touch.

Crane

©S.A.WALTERS

Blue Heron

©S.A.WALTERS

Corners and Borders

Loon

© S.A.WALTERS

Swans

© S.A.WALTERS

White-Tailed Deer

©S.A.WALTERS

Mountain Goat

©S.A.WALTERS

Canada Geese

©S.A.WALTERS

Mallards

©S.A.WALTERS

CHAPTER 8

Hummingbird

Monarch Butterfly

Corners and Borders

103

More Great Books from Fox Chapel Publishing

Celebrating Birch
By The North House Folk School
Includes fascinating birch lore and 20 projects: carved ornaments, turned bowls, bark baskets, and more.

$24.95
ISBN 978-1-56523-307-2

Easy Woodcarving
By Cyndi Joslyn
The only book new woodcarvers need to get started! Learn carving and painting basics with simple techniques and easy projects.

$14.95
ISBN 978-1-56523-288-4

Great Book of Celtic Patterns
By Lora S. Irish
The essential Celtic design reference! Featur 200 original patterns for any medium and the basics to create your ov Celtic art.

$19.95
ISBN 978-1-56523-314-0

Great Book of Woodburning
By Lora S. Irish
Create your own stunning pyrography with techniques, patterns, and easy-to-follow projects.

$19.95
ISBN 978-1-56523-287-7

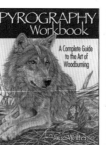

Pyrography Workbook
By Sue Walters
A best-seller! Award-winning artist presents step-by-step projects, original patterns, and an inspiring gallery of work.

$19.95
ISBN 978-1-56523-258-7

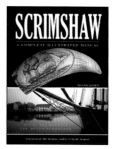

Scrimshaw 2nd Edition
By Steve Paszkiewicz & Roger Schroeder
Discover a classic American art. Includes step-by-step instruction, tool information, patter resource, and gallery.

$14.95
ISBN 978-1-56523-241-9

LOOK FOR THESE BOOKS AT YOUR LOCAL BOOKSTORE OR WOODWORKING RETAILER

Or call 800-457-9112 • Visit www.FoxChapelPublishing.com

Learn from the Experts

You already know that Fox Chapel Publishing is a leading source for woodworking books, videos, and DVDs, but did you know that we also publish two leading magazines in the woodworking category? *Woodcarving Illustrated* and *Scroll Saw Woodworking & Crafts* are the magazines that carving and scroll saw enthusiasts turn to for premium information by today's leading artisans.
Contact us today for your free trial issue!

WOODCARVING
ILLUSTRATED

- Written BY carvers FOR carvers
- Improve your skills with premium carving patterns and step-by-step instruction for all skill levels
- Learn from today's top artists with helpful hints and new techniques for every style of carving
- New product and tool reviews
- Stay in touch with the carving community with biographies, show coverage, a calendar of events, and galleries of completed work

SCROLLSAW
Woodworking & Crafts

- Written by today's leading scroll saw artists
- Dozens of attractive, shop-tested patterns and project ideas for scrollers of all skill levels
- Great full-color photos of step-by-step projects and completed work presented in a clear, easy-to-follow format
- Keep up with what's new in the scrolling community with tool reviews, artist profiles, and event coverage

To Get Your Free Trial Issue or Subscribe:
Call 800-457-9112 or Visit www.FoxChapelPublishing.com